ALL YOU

Spiritual
Healing

VIKAS MALKANI

New Dawn

NEW DAWN
An imprint of Sterling Publishers (P) Ltd.
A-59 Okhla Industrial Area, Phase-II, New Delhi-110020.
Tel: 6912677, 6910050, 6916165, 6916209
Fax: 91-11-6331241 E-mail: ghai@nde.vsnl.net.in
www.sterlingpublishers.com

All you wanted to know about Spiritual Healing
© 2001, Sterling Publishers Private Limited
ISBN 81 207 2396 1

Reprint 2002

Published by Sterling Publishers Pvt. Ltd., New Delhi-110020.
Lasertypeset by Vikas Compographics, New Delhi-110020.
Printed at Sai Printers, New Delhi-110020.

Contents

Disclaimer

The information given here is designed to help you make informed choices and decisions about your health and state of being.

It is not intended as a substitute for any treatment that may have been prescribed by your doctor or physician.

If you have an urgent medical problem, we urge you to seek competent medical help from a qualified practitioner.

All spiritual healing programmes are intended to be complimentary to other systems of medicine and are aimed at both prevention and correction of disease, disharmony and imbalances in the body, mind and spirit trinity.

The author

Introduction

Spiritual healing attempts to heal not only the physical body but also the mind-state and the spiritual self within each individual with the belief that all mental, emotional or physical diseases or illnesses are just symptoms of a much deeper cause. It is the cause that spiritual healing attempts to heal or restore, thereby ending once and for all the symptoms that have been manifested.

The Basis for Spiritual Healing

Spiritual healing works on the foundation of three basic beliefs:

- That the universe and all of creation, is intelligent, is in complete ease, is conscious and harmonious and in balance with its natural state of being

- That man is an integral part of this creation, and thus in his natural state of being possesses the same characteristics.

- That all dis-ease (disharmony) is a manifestation of man's conscious or unconscious separation from this state of universal harmony at any point across the spectrum of his existence. Thus, all diseases are self-manifested and can be healed when a conscious return to harmony is made.

The Requirements for Spiritual Healing

All spiritual healing methods, systems and avenues work on the spirit as well as the mind and body of the practitioner to heal the entire past of his existence and to harmonize his mind, body and spirit. To achieve this goal, requires:

- Faith in the practices or systems he is using - the faith that they will work and produce healing.

Without this faith (i.e. total belief), one will not open up fully, commit fully or give oneself fully to the practice being undertaken; and

- Practice of the system, technique or instruction with dedication, perseverance and patience to allow it to produce its effects in your inner and outer universe.

The Means and Avenues of Spiritual Healing

Since spiritual healing aims to restore the original state of being, ie, a state of complete harmony between the inner and outer being, any system, method, practice or instruction which takes you forward on this path of union and harmony falls under spiritual healing.

The practice of meditation, in its many forms, is the root of spiritual healing.

Alternative systems of healing, such as ayurveda, Reiki, pranic healing, massage therapy, healing through sound, aromatherapy, etc., are also considered valid and valuable systems, each relevant to a different level of healing required.

The practitioner is encouraged in the beginning to attempt or taste those systems to which he/she may be instinctively drawn or attracted and to graduate from there to higher levels of awareness and restoration of health and harmony.

The Author

The Triangle of Spiritual Healing

The Basis and Core Beliefs
of Spiritual Healing

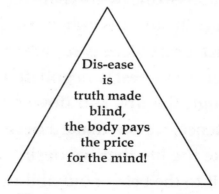

Dis-ease
is
truth made
blind,
the body pays
the price
for the mind!

The
Requirements
for Spiritual Healing

The
Means and Avenues
of Spiritual Healing

What is Self-Healing?

Self-healing is a continual process of taking charge of your health, well-being and personal potential. It comes from actively seeking solutions to the many challenges that we face in our lives rather than seeing ourselves as victims of fate. Instead of doing our best to negotiate a route through the ups and downs of our existence, we can make a decision to create the life that we desire and to live it to the best of our ability.

- Self-healing is using the powers of your mind positively and

12

constructively. To heal and develop your life, you need to be willing to discard the old thoughts, beliefs and attitudes that no longer support you in health and harmony, and exchange them for the new ones that do.

- Self-healing is listening to the intelligence and wisdom of your body. You need to be aware of your physical needs and you need to exercise, feed and think about your body in ways that are loving and healthy.

- Self-healing is harnessing the creative, positive energy of your emotions. You need to be willing to listen to your heart, acknowledge your feelings and express them safely and effectively.

- Self-healing is also about finding your place in the greater scheme of things and developing a philosophy or a spiritual awareness that gives your life a sense of meaning. You need to be willing to expand your view of the world and entertain the joyful mysteries of the universe, regardless of your background, culture or the beliefs that you were brought up with.

It is for you to decide to act upon those choices, but each little step forward, no matter how small, can be a giant leap towards self-healing and personal development.

How Can we Stay Healthy?

Very simply, we stay healthy when we remain in balance. It helps to be in balance with other people and with our environment, but the most important place to start is with ourselves. To be in harmony with the world around us, it is often best to begin by creating harmony within and then work outwards. To have our lives in balance we need to balance ourselves physically, mentally, emotionally and spiritually.

Finding balance is not about sticking to a rigid formula. It is not a case of learning how to do all the right things and holding it there. For example, if you were shown how to place your body in perfect physical alignment, so that your posture was hundred per cent correct, you would have been done a great service. If, however, you were encouraged to hold yourself rigidly in one correct position so that you would never lose that perfect alignment, you would have been done a great disservice. Life is about constant change and movement; being balanced is never going to look quite the same twice.

Remember and use the *four key principles of self-healing*:
- to listen,
- to notice,
- to choose, and
- to adapt.

Listening

Some of us are born with good listening skills; some of us learn them from our parents or parent figures; some of us learn by necessity later on in life. However good a listener you are, there is always something new that you can learn about listening.

Listening is not dependent on our ability to hear. People with impaired hearing can sometimes be better at listening than people whose hearing is clear and perfect.

To heal ourselves we need to listen to our feelings, listen to our bodies, listen to the words that we use, listen to the sound of or feel the vibration of our voices, listen to the information that is coming to us from other people and from our environment. When we listen, we are blessed with all the information that we need to make wonderful healing changes in our lives.

Noticing

When we notice something it often takes on a power or a significance that it did not previously have. When we notice a beautiful flower, a wonderful fragrance or a captivating sound, our mood may change and thoughts, memories or associations may come to mind that were not present before. Similarly, if we notice something unpleasant then it may also take on a significance for us and affect our mood - but by noticing it we can make a choice to change it or, alternatively, to change our response to it.

To heal ourselves we need to be willing to notice our thoughts and beliefs, notice what motivates us and gives us energy, notice what de-motivates us and depletes our energy. It helps to notice the image, inspirations and insights that we receive. Noticing gives us power and helps us to take positive action.

Choosing

So many of us put up with the unsatisfactory or unhealthy elements of our lives because we do not realize that we have the power of choice. We tend to believe that life is something that happens to us regardless of our wishes, dreams or desires, and we often picture ourselves as victims of circumstance doing our best to cope with the hand that we have been dealt.

When we learn that we have a choice and that we have a right to exercise that choice in all areas of our health and happiness, we discover that we have the power to make wonderful changes.

To heal ourselves we often need to choose new ways of thinking and acting. This includes choosing new ways to look at life, choosing to let go of anything that no longer supports our health and happiness and choosing new directions that will enhance our personal development. When we exercise our choice we create new options for ourselves and we take charge of our destiny.

Adapting

Some illnesses and many problems are created as a direct result of our basic fear and resistance to life. Even the most positive people may fear or resist some areas of change. In contrast, some of the healthiest people have been those with a great willingness to adapt and learn new ways of approaching life.

To heal ourselves we often need to adapt to changing circumstances: adapting to different environments, adapting to changing needs and desires, adapting our approach to obtain the best results in all situations, adapting ideas, techniques, treatments and philosophies. When we are willing to adapt, we remain flexible and open to solutions that go beyond our previous expectations or experience.

When we continue to listen, notice, choose and adapt, then we are able to create and recreate balance within ourselves, allowing our passage through life to be as healthy and happy as it was always meant to be.

The Message of Illness

While it is always preferable to stay balanced and prevent illness from occurring as much as possible, the advent of illness can be a gift, especially when we choose to look at our situation positively and with love. It is true that we may not feel that our illness is a blessing when it is painful or uncomfortable and when it inhibits us from living life to the full, but we still have it within our

24

power to turn it into a beneficial gift rather than a curse.

Illness always brings a message. Physical symptoms tell us that there is something we need to learn about ourselves and something we need to change. The message may be a predominantly physical one. If we have a backache then the message might be that we need to learn to move in a different way or that we need to learn to stand correctly. Listening to your body and noticing aches and pains early can allow you to choose new ways of correcting them by finding out about, for example, appropriate exercise, therapies and postural training. Even if you begin to take heed of the aches after some damage has already occurred, there is much you can do to improve the situation and prevent further deterioration.

With physical symptoms, however, the message may also be emotional. The backache that requires us to move, lift and stand in a healthier way also requires us to look at the cause of the emotional tension that is contributing to the pain or the discomfort we are experiencing. Alternatively, the message may be a mental one: perhaps we are viewing ourselves and our lives in ways that rigidly adhere to old patterns of belief that no longer suit us. Rigid thinking is one cause of rigidity within the body; the pain may be telling us that we need to change the way we view our current situation.

A Spiritual Perspective

We are more than just a body, a collection of emotions and a series of thoughts. The more that I learn about the nature of self-healing, the more I am convinced that the most profound transformation occurs when we are willing to acknowledge that there is a greater aspect of ourselves.

Imagine that there is a part of you that sees the bigger picture of your life and is able to direct you towards your highest joy. This part of you is quite different from your conscious mind, which appears to be directing everything during your waking hours. This part of you is able to see beyond the mental limitations that you place upon yourself and if you allow it to, will help you to stay healthy and happy.

It is not important whether we have a firm spiritual belief that this is the part of ourselves connected to God, or instead take a less spiritually-based view of life and see this greater aspect of ourselves as an area of our minds that we have yet to learn more about; either way we can learn to work with our greater awareness to help us heal ourselves.

Some people call it the higher self, the higher mind or the god-self. Others may describe it as their over-soul, greater consciousness or higher wisdom. It really does not matter what we call it, how it fits into our religious or spiritual philosophy, or even if we hold a firm belief that it exists, just being willing to entertain the possibility that there is a wise spiritual being inside each of us can bring dramatic changes.

For some of us, healing occurs when our symptoms disappear and their underlying causes dissolve; for others, healing is concerned with reaching a greater understanding of themselves and finding grace and dignity as they come to terms with their illness or their death. Whatever our path, our greater awareness can help us to make sense of what is happening to us and put our lives into perspective.

The Spiritual Purpose of Illness

Some of us create illness or problems as a way of directing ourselves towards our greatest joy. It may not always feel like this at moments when we are in pain or dealing with symptoms that restrict our mobility and impede our lives, but so many people grow through their illnesses, becoming more aware of themselves, more mature and often more spiritually focused. It helps when we can begin to view everything that happens to us, as an opportunity rather than a disaster.

Illness is not an essential part of our growth and development; it is just one way that we express and resolve our inner conflicts and move ourselves towards our higher potential. Often we can prevent illness and accelerate healing by being willing to find other ways to grow and integrate our spiritual lessons. You can begin by asking yourself the question, *'How can I best move beyond my old limitations to become all that I was created to be?'*

Exercise: The message of illness
Find somewhere quiet and comfortable to sit and have a pen and paper on hand. Start by sitting with your body open and relaxed. Close your eyes and breathe deeply, just as you would if you were beginning a visualization. In your mind, ask for help in locating and releasing the underlying cause of any illness or ailments that you are currently dealing with.

Ask too for new ways to deal with any long-term conditions or recurring problems, and declare that you are available for transformational changes of attitude. When you feel centred and ready, open your eyes and write your instinctive answers to the following questions:

- *What have my problems or illness got to teach me at this time?*
- *What do I need to learn that will aid my happiness and well-being?*
- *What is the underlying message of my illness/problems?*
- *What do I need to do, to release my condition or problems and move on?*

Do your best not to judge or limit the answers that you receive, even if they do not make sense to you at this time. Do not worry if you do not receive any insights immediately. It is often enough to ask the right questions for the process of healing to be set in motion. Also, allowing yourself to answer instinctively can take practice. Make sure that you act upon any relevant ideas, and complete the process by affirming:

- I AM WILLING TO FOLLOW MY UNIQUE SPIRITUAL PATH.
- I AM AVAILABLE FOR MY HIGHEST GOOD.

- I AM ALWAYS GUIDED TOWARDS HEALTH AND JOY.

Repeat this exercise regularly, staying open to new insights and new changes of attitude that could make a difference to your ongoing process of self-healing.

Creating a Life With Purpose

The healthiest people are often those who create for themselves a life of meaning and purpose. If we have a vision of what we wish to create, things that we want to do and an opportunity to contribute something of ourselves to the world around us, then we tend to be supported in health, happiness and spiritual growth. Older people who stay healthy and animated long after they have passed retirement age are often those who actively seek new things to learn and new ways to contribute to others.

We sometimes expect life to provide us with a purpose or meaning and we wait for other people to take the initiative of inviting us to participate in our own personal development. The truth is that we are always invited to take part in the adventure of life, but it is up to us to seize that opportunity. If your life does not appear to have a meaning, create one for yourself.

If you are lacking direction then take some time to listen to your underlying purpose. The clues are always there. *What motivates you? What inspires you? What do you desire? What engages your interest?* The things that we feel passionate about act as the road signs for our healing journey. They tell us where we need to go to fulfil our spiritual purpose.

Seeing the Bigger Picture

We are usually so immersed in the day-to-day dramas of our lives that we do not see the bigger picture. We rush around doing our best to fulfil all of our commitments, take care of the people whom we love, stay financially solvent and deal with our physical or emotional challenges, and in doing so, we forget that there may be a greater purpose to our lives. We forget to look at our overall direction, neglecting to draw a distinction between the things that we do out of habit, guilt or a lack of imagination and the things that we do because they actively move our lives forward.

Sometimes we emerge from our routines and dramas to see our lives with greater clarity. We are suddenly able to make sense of our experiences and see the obvious solutions to the challenges we are facing. At these times of clarity we may gain great insight into the meaning and purpose of everything that is happening to us; we may even develop a sense of divine inspiration. An example is when we suddenly understand in our hearts something that we have understood intellectually for some time and have not been able to apply. Grasping the feeling of something rather than just the ideas, can make a transformational difference to us.

Some illnesses provide us with a bridge to the bigger picture of our lives. At times we create illnesses as a way of diverting ourselves from a path we are taking that no longer serves us and on to a new one that will allow us to grow. At other times we use them to slow ourselves down so that we can allow space for our dreams, desires and inner feelings to direct us beyond our old limiting beliefs.

The Intelligence of Your Body

The Power of Your Body

Our bodies have an extraordinary capacity for self-healing. Whether we are sleeping or awake and preoccupied with the details of our day, our bodies are taking care of the digestion and assimilation of food, the elimination of waste matter, the assimilation of oxygen from the air and the continual regeneration of cells. There are many things that our bodies have to deal with, from infections to sprains and from cuts to bruises which in numerous cases will get better regardless of the treatments that we use. Our bodies know how to heal and regenerate themselves; they have their own intelligence.

Even in cases of disability or some long-term conditions that disrupt certain functions, the intelligence of the body is still able to take care of an incredible number of sophisticated tasks, and can make a significant difference to the speed of our recuperation, and ability to stay as healthy and comfortable as possible.

Getting in the Way

Perhaps the main challenge that the body is likely to face as it goes about the business of regenerating itself comes from within. We have learned to get in the way of the body's natural ability to heal, obstructing many of its normal functions and inhibiting its natural rhythms and timings. How you think about your body and how you treat it, often disrupts its ability to function as efficiently as it can.

In many cases, we have become quite separated from our bodies. So much emphasis is placed upon our ability to think in logical, reasonable ways, to the exclusion of our intuition and gut awareness, that we cut off from much of the physical information that we receive. Intelligence has become chiefly associated with intellect; we have forgotten that our bodies also have intelligence. Harnessing that intelligence, listening to it, acknowledging it and responding to it, are essential to self-healing.

Many of us have learned to hate our bodies. We send our bodies messages of self-loathing, abuse and mistrust. We have learned to fear our sexuality, despise the way that we look and criticize our bodies for their failings rather than acknowledge their strengths. We say things like, '*I hate my thighs,*' '*My body is always letting me down*' and '*I hate the way that I look.*' Apart from the negative energy of all those negative thoughts, we give our bodies specific messages that they respond to. Is it any wonder that they sometimes respond with weakness, disharmony or disease?

We abuse our bodies with alcohol, nicotine and other recreational drugs and expect them to function perfectly. The remarkable thing is that they often do, making an incredible effort to adjust to the effects of these poisonous substances and eliminate them from our systems. However, the more we abuse out bodies in this way, the more their abilities to regenerate or bounce back decreases.

We abuse our bodies with food. We eat too much or too little, at odd or irregular times of the day, too much junk food, or processed food, or too many food items that our bodies are intolerant to or allergic to. This, however does not mean that there is one ideal diet for us all because our bodies have their own needs and rhythms. What is an excellent diet for one person may be quite wrong for another. What is more, our bodies may have different needs at different times during our lives; we would benefit from listening to these changing needs, noticing the impact that foods have upon us, choosing to eat the foods that our bodies want and adapting our habits and life-style accordingly.

As a general rule, we are more likely to stay healthy when we have regular meal-times, eat wholefoods rather than junk, eat fresh foods rather than processed, tinned or frozen ones, eat lots of fresh vegetables and fruits, eat a balance of raw and cooked foods and avoid eating lots of cheese, red meat and processed sugar.

Even the way that we think about what we eat can make a difference. If we think about our food positively before we put it in our mouths, our bodies can respond to it in a healthier way. However, even these general guidelines are not right for everyone; each of us needs to experiment for ourselves.

We do not exercise our bodies enough or we exercise them in the wrong way. It is just as unhealthy to have a static lifestyle as it is to 'go for the burn'. It often works best to have a mixture of different kinds of exercise, some gentle, some more vigorous, some more contemplative, some more upbeat and fun. Walking is excellent; oriental systems such as yoga or tai chi are second to none when properly taught; swimming improves stamina and lung capacity; aerobic dance classes and weight-training sessions are also fine when properly supervised and when not taken to extremes. As with diet, we need to experiment and find out what suits our bodies.

Learning to Love Your Body

The best way to change our habits is to start by learning to think about our bodies in a different way. Bodies that are thought about and talked about with love are much more likely to respond with health and balance. Rather than spend time talking or thinking about the ways in which your body fails you, which produces negative energy, you can place your attention on the many successes of your body and give energy to the things that it does well. In this way you can redirect that negative energy into positive energy.

If we constantly think about our bodies as unreliable, ugly, hateful and inadequate, then we significantly contribute to patterns of disharmony and deterioration. If, on the other hand, we acknowledge the changes that we would like to make in our physical state while loving and accepting our bodies as they are now, praising them for the many ways in which they function well and doing our best to take care of them, we will significantly contribute to new patterns of health, well-being and beauty. Our bodies are meant to be different, we are all unique – but we all have one thing in common: when we learn to love and take care of our bodies we can increase their ability to function well. Some of us are meant to be fatter than others, some of us are born with disabilities that are not going to go away, but the way that we think about them and act towards them can be transformational.

We can support our bodies in finding their ideal, healthy weight, increasing their range of mobility, staying comfortable and pain-free and giving us a great deal of pleasure.

Here are some guidelines to help you love your body:

- Refuse to compare your body to others. We are often taught to be quite critical of our appearance by comparing ourselves to other people. We learn to look at somebody else and either feel superior or inadequate, depending upon how we rate our appearance or our capabilities against theirs. If we are looking for it, there is always someone who is going to appear more beautiful, more handsome, fatter, thinner, stronger, more agile or more able than us; the ultimate pay-off is that we get to feel bad about ourselves and hate our bodies.

As mentioned earlier, your body is unique. If you refuse to enter into judgements and comparisons you will allow yourself to enjoy the beauty and brilliance of your body, encouraging it to grow in health, strength and capability.

- Look at your body in a full-length mirror and notice your thoughts and reactions. This is most effective when you are naked. *Does your mind immediately become critical? Do you look for distractions and tear yourself away from your image as soon as you can? Does it upset, distress or disappoint you when you look at any area of your body, such as your thighs, your arms, your wrinkles, your spots or your damaged leg?*

Practise looking at yourself with as much love as you can. Talk to your body using words of love and respect. Even if it seems strange or a silly thing to do at first, you will benefit from looking at your reflection and saying to yourself:

I Love My Body.

I Love My Chest/Arms/Thighs/Skin, etc.

I Ask My body to stay Healthy.

I Thank My Body For Staying Healthy.

- Learn to touch yourself with tenderness and love. Do not hit yourself, even in jest, as you could be reinforcing abusive patterns of thought and behaviour from your past.

- Learn to think positively about your sexuality. Most of us have picked up some negative baggage about sex and sexuality during our lives. Perhaps we have learned to fear our bodies and the sexual feelings that we have. Perhaps we picked up our parents' discomfort in talking about sex, or we may feel guilty for enjoying the pleasure of our bodies.

Learning to Listen to Your Body
In choosing the appropriate diet, exercise programme, treatments and remedies, it helps to learn to listen to your body. Listening to the messages that our bodies are giving us takes practice because we have actively learned lifestyles, beliefs and patterns

of behaviour that block those messages and keep us in ignorance. Those messages may seem subtle and intangible in comparison to the information that we process in our brains, but they are still powerful and can tell us a lot about our health and well-being.

When we are actively listening to our bodies, we are more able to pick up the early clues to areas of imbalance or disharmony. Acting on that information we can adjust our behaviour or our lifestyle to help prevent illness or greater problems from occurring. A simple example of this is listening to and acknowledging our tiredness and taking a rest when our bodies want to.

Another set of messages that we have learned to ignore are those that come from our stomachs. Some of us carry on working all day without food, despite the fact that our stomachs are telling us to eat. Many more of us eat and continue to eat when we are not hungry, ignoring signals that we are full, bloated or even nauseated. In some cases we eat out of habit, in others we eat for emotional reasons, stuffing down feelings of fear, anger, joy and passion rather than acknowledging them. Linked with this, we often eat because we are looking for some form of instant gratification.

When we listen to our bodies, we can also learn to detect the underlying emotional, mental or spiritual causes of physical problems. Physical pain, for example, may be telling us that there is something physically wrong but it may also be telling us that we have some unexpressed emotional pain that we need to acknowledge and address.

The intelligence of the body is quite extraordinary. Our bodies hold memories of everything that has ever happened to us. They retain the joyful memories and the painful ones, they remember the feelings and the actions, the experiences and the effects of those experiences; they hold an imprint that is not dissimilar to a three-dimensional photograph.

The Wisdom of Your Emotions

The Power of Your Emotions

Just as your body has its own intelligence, so have your emotions. Our emotions are a constant source of energy, creativity and personal power that can be tapped for self-healing. They have their own wisdom, rhythm and timing which, given the right conditions, can help to keep us healthy. It is our feelings that bring colour into our lives. We are motivated by our passions or our anger, lifted by our joy, depressed by our sadness and inspired by our capacity to love.

It is the misuse, misdirection and suppression of our emotional energy, that contributes to many illnesses and relationship problems. We have learned to restrict some of our feelings and distort others with our negative or limiting beliefs so that they either become overly controlled or out of control. Emotions that are not expressed or that become over-emphasized can create a physical imbalance and affect our ability to communicate our true needs and desires.

Our Emotional Education

As we grow up, we learn not only a vast vocabulary of thoughts and beliefs but also about the expression of emotions. In most cases, babies are emotionally straightforward. When they are happy, they gurgle with delight; when they are distressed or angry, they yell and scream. Their communication is essentially simple, direct and effective. They give clear signals to their parents or parent figures whenever they are content or uncomfortable, hungry or in need of attention. It is only as they grow and develop, that their emotional lives become more complex.

As children, we copy the emotional behaviour that we observe around us. If our parents are good at expressing anger but not very good at expressing love or sadness, it is likely that we will develop similar emotional patterns. If our parents approve of us when we are all smiles but ignore us when we are tearful or angry, then we will learn to wear a smile regardless of our underlying feelings.

Our vocabulary of beliefs and our patterns of emotional behaviour are often inextricably linked. We pick up direct judgements about our emotions and we learn to think about our feelings in ways that inhibit them, deny them or over-emphasize them. This is how we create the conflict between the head, the heart and the voice of our inner self. We have feelings and desires but our beliefs do not give us permission to have them and so our expression becomes suppressed or distorted.

For example, as children we may have demonstrated a high level of joy and passion that was considered to be unacceptable. We may have been naturally enthusiastic people whose parents were not in touch with their own enthusiasm and excitement and who therefore had a problem handling ours.

Children can become passionately joyful about anything from a beautiful flower to a wonderful new toy and from a new way of playing a game to a visit from Grandma. Perhaps that enthusiasm needs safe boundaries so that it does not become entirely disruptive or inappropriate to the situation. But it also needs to be encouraged, accepted and approved of, so that it can contribute to a lifetime of safe, joyful pleasure.

Parents who were not given permission to be joyful and

passionate when they were children do not always know how to give their own children that permission. Parents who were not taught how to accept their anger and express it safely are often unable to pass these skills on to their children. People whose own parents were not very permissive and accepting of their sadness, disappointment, anger distress or grief do not necessarily have the experience to permit these feelings in their children, unless they have learned to break free of their conditioning and liberate themselves from their families' emotional patterns.

In some cases, the beliefs and patterns of behaviour that we learn leave us unable to recognize many of our feelings. As children, when we become angry or too demanding we are often told that we are tired. Sometimes this is true and sometimes not; it is just easy to label demanding behaviour as tiredness than to acknowledge the needs or feelings that are present. As adults, we may not think of ourselves as being particularly emotional but every time we become angry or have needs to be addressed we may find ourselves becoming sleepy. We have learned that it is safer to become unconscious than to address our emotions.

Sometimes it is valuable to look back to childhood and remind ourselves where some of our beliefs or emotional patterns came from. Looking back at the past can give us insights about the choices that we have made and help us to make new choices and amend the wrong ones in our lives right now. It does not help to look back to the past with the intention to blame our parents, families, teachers or friends for the problems that we have had in our lives. Nor does it serve our process of self-healing to blame ourselves for past choices and mistakes. We simply need to look for inofrmation that will broaden our understanding, help us to leave the past behind and create something totally different in the present and the future.

The Emotional Nature of Illness

What do our illnesses say about our emotional state and our ability to express our feelings? Certainly, a person's emotional state needs to be considered in all areas of healing; if there is illness or imbalance, then there is generally an emotional factor that needs to be acknowledged and addressed. In some cases, the emotions are major contributors to the condition or the problem; in other cases they are not a significant part of the initial cause, but they become significant once the first symptoms have been established.

Illness can be said to be an expression of an inner conflict. When there is an underlying mental, emotional or spiritual tension that affects our well-being, we seek to express, resolve and release that tension in the best way that we know how. If we have not learned to do it in any other way, we do it by creating symptoms. A symptom is a signal that there is some underlying imbalance; it is an indication to ourselves and to others that we need some care and attention. It is rare for the cause of that imbalance to be purely physical.

Emotion and Injury

We often consider our injuries to be purely physical. We cut our finger, break a leg or damage our spine in an accident and we can clearly pinpoint a physical reason for our problem. However, our mental and emotional state could also have contributed to our initial injury and could well be contributing to the rate of our recovery and our ability to manage our symptoms.

The timing of an injury is often significant, and it is always useful to ask yourself what was going on in your life at the time when you injured yourself; what was happening around you and what were your underlying thoughts and feelings? The timing of your recovery is also significant. What is happening around you and inside you as your pain diminishes or your body repairs itself?

Emotion and Disease

All the diseases and infections that we create in our bodies have their mental and emotional factors. It is always valid to ask yourself what the beliefs and emotions are that are contributing to this condition; what changes of belief will help you to heal this and what emotions you need to acknowledge and express, in order to help heal yourself?

When we are sick, the first emotional clues that we have, are the feelings that go hand in hand with our symptoms. We can ask ourselves how this illness makes us feel — if your cold makes you feel sad then it is valid to assume that some previously unexpressed sadness has contributed to the creation of your condition. Colds are often means of detoxifying ourselves. They help to clear our bodies of accumulated junk and our emotional selves of unexpressed feelings. They also help to clear the tension caused by negative and invalidating thoughts.

If you have a cold, trust the feelings that you have and work with them rather than deny them.

Similarly, if we develop a more extreme condition, such as a form of cancer, it is important that we work with our thoughts and feelings. If our response to our diagnosis is shock, anger and grief then it would be worth exploring these feelings further, as they may have contributed to the creation of the condition and may well contribute to some healing solutions. A willingness to acknowledge our emotions could powerfully support the effectiveness of our chosen treatments and help to prevent a reoccurrence of the disease. Many forms of cancer are related to some powerful, unexpressed feelings, particularly anger.

Our emotions do have their own wisdom. When we trust them and give ourselves permission to have them then they help us to heal. Emotions are creative energy; when we acknowledge them, express them and release them they can help us to create wonderful experiences in our lives, bringing colour to our relationships and motivation to our spiritual purpose. When we deny them, hold on to them or build them up out of all proportion with negative or fearful thoughts, then we risk turning that creative energy back on itself, and that is when they contribute to disease and disharmony.

Emotions and Long-term Illness

With long-term illness it becomes even more essential to remain emotionally open and fluid. The prevention of further deterioration and the successful management of symptoms are greatly helped by the ongoing management and healing of emotions. When, for instance, we have weak spots in our bodies from old injuries or debilitating disease, we may experience a level of physical pain that is directly related to the condition itself, although the extent of the pain that we feel may be greatly increased by mental and emotional factors. Unexpressed emotional pain is often felt as additional physical pain, as are mental patterns of self-punishment, self-criticism and guilt. Simply put, our unresolved issues and unexpressed feelings have a tendency to settle in our physical weak spots.

Painkilling drugs are a miracle of the modern age that allow many people to live with dignity and in relative comfort. However they are often over-used. Pain is a warning that there is something wrong, it indicates that there is something that we need to change or resolve. Listening to the pain and working with it can help us to make the physical, mental and emotional changes necessary to heal the cause of the pain or at least diminish it. When we knock out the pain with drugs, we may detach ourselves from the underlying cause of the pain and therefore cut ourselves off from potential healing solutions.

With long-term illnesses that bring continual pain, we need to make the appropriate choices about effective pain management but we also need to listen to ourselves so that we are continuing to address any underlying emotional and psychological issues. This may mean getting appropriate medical advice about reducing painkillers and supplementing with relaxation techniques, regular sessions with a spiritual healer, counselling or complementary therapies. Let us manage our pain without deadening our self-healing power.

One of the most effective ways to stimulate a process of emotional healing is to bring acceptance and forgiveness to our illness or problem. It may seem a strange idea to 'forgive' your disease or 'learn to love' your condition, but our illnesses and problems represent a part of ourselves that needs our acceptance in order to heal. The energy used in hating or despising our condition has a tendency to keep us attached to it, whereas the energy of love brings transformation.

Seven Misconceptions About the Human Body

We suffer from seven illusions about the body. These misconceptions profoundly affect the way we relate to our body and to other beings.

- *The body is solid.* In reality, most of the body is sheer vacuum.

- *The body is individuated.* In reality, we are in constant molecular exchange with other bodies, which makes nonsense out of the common presumption that a particular body is ours.

- *The body is stable*. In reality, our body is constantly changing. Every five years, all the cells have been replaced.
- *The body is stationary*. In reality, our body is never still but continuously in motion, together with all the other bodies, small or large, in the universe.
- *The body belongs to the Earth*. In reality, the human body is made not simply of the maternal ovum and the paternal sperm, but of the high energy material present fourteen billion years ago.
- *The body is mindless*. In reality, far from being unconscious, our body

84

is endowed with sentience apart from the functions of the brain. In other words, the brain is not the only "mindful" organ of the body. Tissues and organs far removed from the brain seem to have brainlike properties as well.

- *The body is me.* In reality, we are neither the body nor anything it contains — the breath, the mind, the thoughts, the emotions and the desires. We are what sustains all this and pervades it.

Yoga for Healthy Living

The ancient yogis recognized long ago that in order to accomplish the highest goal of yoga, which is the realization of the self, or God consciousness, a healthy physical body is essential. When we are sick, our attention is seldom free enough to contemplate the larger reality, or to muster the energy for practice.

The masters of yoga also teach us that personal growth is possible only when we fully accept our embodiment and when we truly understand that the body is not merely skin and bones but a finely balanced system of energies.

Although yoga is best used as preventive medicine, some of its practices also have great therapeutic value. They can help those suffering from various difficult physical conditions, like back pain, scoliosis, and arthritis. However, ideally, your yoga practice should be an integral part of your efforts to maintain good health and prevent degenerative disease.

Therapeutic Yoga

The word "therapy" comes from the Greek word *therapeuein*, meaning "to heal, to take care of". Yoga can be understood as a comprehensive approach to healing, for it goes to the root of all diseases, which is our false relationship to life itself. We fall ill when our body or mind is out of balance. Ultimately, there can be no complete healing until we have restored our primal trust in life, which alone removes all those obstructions within us that tend to manifest as ill health.

Most of our diseases are symptoms of an underlying disease: our sense of being cut off from the sustaining power of life. We feel separated, isolated, alienated and ill. As we become aware of this feeling, which we share with billions of others, we experience the need for wholeness. We begin to understand that we are not really sealed off from life but are in fact interconnected with everything and everyone else. At times, this intellectual understanding may be confirmed and enriched by an actual experience of unity and wholeness.

The word 'yoga' is a very ancient Sanskrit word. It is derived from the root 'Yuk' — meaning "to join, to unite!"

Yoga seeks to restore the condition of wholeness in which, even if we should experience a spell of misfortune and illness, we nevertheless feel restored to life and healed in our relationship to the larger reality. Yoga is radical spiritual therapy.

For millennia, yoga has had a close connection with *ayurveda,* which is India's traditional medical and healing system. According to Ayurveda, which literally means "science of life", body and mind form an interactive system. This is also the viewpoint of yoga. Both schools of thought also insist that a healthy, wholesome life must be happy and morally sound. Moreover, the authorities of Ayurveda and yoga recommend the cultivation of self-knowledge and serenity, which ensure our well-being.

Western medicine is slowly rediscovering these ancient fundamental insights about disease, health, and wholeness.

There is growing literature on Ayurveda, traditional Chinese medicine, homeopathy, herbalism, aromatherapy, colour therapy, body-work, healing touch, and so on. More than ever, we do not need to be passive victims of our illness or of the currently available knowledge of our present medical system.

Prayer is Powerful Medicine

A well-known study by Randolph Byrd made headlines a couple of years ago.

Health Practices, Attitudes and Immunity

Enhances Immune Function	Depresses Immune Function
Health Practices	
Good nutrition	Poor diet (poor quality, improper quantity)
Proper exercise	Inactivity
Adequate sleep	Insomnia, somnolence
Relaxation, meditation	Constant stress
Breathing practice or paced respiration	Smoking, heavy alcohol consumption
Approach to Life	
Active approach to illness	Resigned, helpless approach to illness

Cont.

Health Practices, Attitudes and Immunity

Optimistic, positive outlook	Pessimism
Change seen as opportunity for growth	Change seen as threat
Internal locus of control	External locus of control
Inner stability, equanimity	Agitation, emotional volatility
Appropriate self-confidence	Too much or too little self-confidence
Sense of purpose, commitment	Apathy
Social support system	Isolation
Involvement	Alienation
Warm relationship with others	Poor communication with others

Byrd was a cardiologist at San Francisco General Hospital who decided to do a study on the efficacy of prayer. He took 500 patients who had been admitted to the coronary intensive care unit, either for heart attack or to rule out heart attack, and he had them randomly assigned to a prayed-for and a not-prayed-for group.

It was the pinnacle of controlled scientific research, a randomized double blind study. None of the staff knew who was in which group so they could not preferentially give care to one group and not the other, and the subjects were chosen at random, so factors like sex, age, health and demographics would balance out. Then he farmed out their names to prayer groups of various denominations around the country.

When they broke the code at the end of the study, they found that indeed the prayed-for patients did significantly better on a number of measures. They got fewer infections, needed fewer antibiotics, got out of the hospital sooner. No one in the prayed-for group needed a respirator, whereas 16 or 17 of the others did.

The differences were so significant that if prayer had been a drug, there would have been a run on the market for it. One well-known debunker of similar studies could find absolutely nothing wrong with this one. "Now I can truly say," he wrote, "that physicians should take out their pads and write prescriptions for prayer."

There is no way to explain these results in terms of a brain generating consciousness in the body. The only way to explain it is that somehow the thoughts of one person can affect another person at a distance.

Tips for Healthy Nutrition

- Increase fruits, vegetables and whole grains in your diet.

- Reduce processed foods, which contain additives and preservatives that have little nutritional value and in the long run have a toxic effect on the body.

- Reduce your consumption of fats to no more than 20-30 per cent of your daily calories.

- Reduce your intake of sugar and sugar-loaded foods.

- Reduce your intake of salt and overly salty foods.

- Eliminate caffeine from your diet, whether in coffee or chocolate.

- Drink plenty of pure water.

- Do not eat when you are stressed-out or aggravated. Wait until you are calm again.
- Prepare your meals so that they look inviting.
- Eat consciously, with enjoyment
- Do not overeat.
- Once a week have nothing but a fruit juice or vegetable juice, which will help to clean your system.

The Basis and Benefits of Mantra Healing

A *mantra* is a syllable, a word or a set of words of immense spiritual power, handed down in a spiritual tradition for many years.

The repetition of a mantra is a means of improving the powers of concentration. There are Indian spiritual masters who maintain that the meaning and the content of the mantra do not necessarily have to be understood by the aspirant in order to bring about the desired effect. That the practice of mantra alone is sufficient to achieve the spiritual awakening, which is its purpose.

Certainly, the use of mantra purifies the subconscious. Even if it is repeated mechanically some purification will take place. However, each mantra is devotional by nature and has the divine as its form and essence. With concentration on the meaning, the attainment of the ultimate goals is surer and quicker.

The benefits of mantra practice depends on you as an individual, on where you started off, where you stand now, what your past life has been, and the intensity and degree of longing in your desire.

When you chant a mantra your whole being changes for the better.

One of the results that comes quickly with the practice of mantra is control of the breath, which is the means by which we can develop the ability to control the emotions. In chanting, we can give all our emotions to the mantra, to the deity of the mantra, and ask that deity to help us gain control. In this way we find a safe release for negative feelings. Rather than throwing them on someone else, we offer them back to their source. Continued chanting will lead to greater awareness and replacing of negative feelings with positive affirmations.

Mantra practice calms down the turbulent emotions and the turbulent mind. In yogic terms there is a difference between emotions and feelings, since a purified emotion becomes a true feeling. Mantra yoga gives us an opportunity to know the emotions, what they are, where they come from, and what is their proper place in our lives. Through mantra yoga we can learn to deal with our emotions properly, to control and refine them, and to encourage the harmonious development of all aspects of human potential.

As the mantra is put into the subconscious, the mind is purified to the extent that we would be incapable without this aid. Slowly the ego is overpowered by the higher self. As it purifies the mind, the mantra is also a great protection from fear.

When emotions are purified they develop into love, which is an important step in the awakening of further levels of consciousness, and the influence of the mantra becomes very subtle. Feelings which have been purified bring us into the presence of the divine and from the divine we feel a sense of protection. The mantra is like a shield against all that is negative and disturbing.

The voice can become an instrument for expressing and controlling the emotions. At times your chanting may be caressing, gentle, intense, full of longing or surrender. If you chant softly, you may observe that your emotions become more gentle. They will become refined through the chanting, and change into true feelings which are expressed in the heart. At other times your voice may be strong and powerful as you put into it all your anger and disappointment, your requests and demands. Honestly express to God what you feel, even your anger and impatience towards the divine for not bringing you sooner to the light. However, you must also learn when to stop expressing emotions or your practice will become emotional self-indulgence.

When you find that your emotions are extremely difficult to control, you may give them back to the divine at a very personal level, saying, "*Why did you give me all these emotions? Why did you not give me strength and insight to handle them? I want you to come here now and do something about it."* This may not seem like a form of prayer, but it is. It is the recognition of the need for help and the willingness to ask God for that help, and that is humility.

In chanting out the emotions, from the ugliest to the most exalted, and giving them back to the one who gave them to you in the first place, you learn to accept both parts of yourself, the good and the bad, and to transcend the pairs of opposites, from which we are trying to free ourselves. On the spiritual path, by channeling the emotions towards God, we find that the divine accepts our struggle, and aids as well as sustains us in our search for the most high.

Emotions in themselves are not bad, but when running wild they can be extremely damaging. Even love , when not shared, not given freely and generously, becomes self-love which turns destructively back on the individual. When emotions are directed, they are the source of strength for great achievements. Through the power of emotions men and women have overcome their limitations and attained a higher purpose in life. Emotions channelled through a mantra towards the Divine can take you close to God.

When chanting a mantra the emotions express themselves in the breath and voice. Every time the breath is uneven it means the emotions are involved and we are out of balance. As long as the emotions are running high, this imbalance exists, but gradually they subside and we begin to experience the equilibrium that is our goal.

Chanting helps us to achieve this silence by bringing the breath and the emotions under control. In these moments of complete stillness of the mind, indescribable bliss is experienced. By repeated practice it becomes possible to hold onto the contact made with our innermost being.

As the mantra is chanted, moods will, in time, be brought under control and awareness of the present will grow. Attention, and therefore energy, will be withdrawn from the old thought patterns, which like tapes on a tape recorder, play over and over. These mental background noises keep us tied to the past and future, to fearful imagining and senseless fantasies, which cause our self-created sufferings.

The ability to concentrate, to achieve single-pointedness, and the overcoming of self will go hand-in-hand. Through the practice of mantra and Japa yoga you will find yourself in direct confrontation with the lower self, the ego or body/mind. You will become aware of those personality aspects that have been in control and have ruled your life. Now the higher self begins to take possession.

To overcome the ego one must practise surrender. One must be able to surrender to the mantra itself and to the energy of the mantra which puts in motion the process of purification of the self, facing up to and eliminating selfishness, self-glorification, self-justification, and self-gratification.

If you go to bed at night and fall asleep with the mantra, it will probably stay with you and you will wake up with it. You will have no dreams, because the generative power of the mantra dissolves problems and removes the pressures that come from self-importance and self-will.

Through the use of mantra a greater sensitivity, a refinement of the senses, comes about which may eventually bring you to the point where you can see with the inner eye and hear with the inner ear. When the inner ear is developed, the music of the spheres may be heard, music of such exquisite beauty as no instrument, no human voice, is able to produce. The cosmic AUM might be heard. The impact and effects of such experiences will bring an intense desire to change for the better.

Mantra is not a magic pill; rather it is like a steady stream of water which gradually wears down the hardest stone. The immediate results of chanting are an increase in the ability to concentrate, followed gradually by control of the breath and the emotions. Later the emotions will become refined into true feelings. The most important goal in chanting, however, is the realization of the self.

The Path of Healing

Enlightenment is oneness, beyond grasping at self, beyond duality, beyond happy or sad, beyond positive or negative *karma*. However, when we talk of healing it is not necessary to be too concerned with enlightenment. Realizing the true nature of our minds is the ultimate healing, but the ordinary mind also has healing powers. We can use our everyday, dualistic minds to help ourselves. Most exercises take this everyday approach to become more relaxed and happy.

So our aim is simply to go from negative to positive, from sickness to healing. If we are already in a positive state for the time being, we can learn how to maintain and enjoy that. However, the more we loosen our grasping, that much better we will feel.

On a long journey, we may want to keep the ultimate destination in mind, but it is good to take one day at a time and rest along the way. If we want to relax our grip on self, we should not try too hard. It is better to take a gentle approach. Whatever steps we take, even if they are small, the most important thing is to rejoice in those small steps, then they become powerful. We should always appreciate what we are able to do, and not feel bad about what we have not done.

If we are newcomers to meditation and spiritual training, it is important to be practical, to use our knowledge of ourselves to take the right path. When we keep an open attitude, specific healing meditations can help us swiftly along the path. The best guide of all is the wisdom within us. We are not restricted to a few methods of meditation. Instead, all of life — thinking, feeling, everyday activities and experiences can be a means of healing.

Avoidance

A word about avoidance. Usually we face problems in order to heal them, but not always. Sometimes the best approach is avoidance. For example, if your problem is mild or temporary, not a deep-rooted habit or a feeling of severe pain, ignoring it will be a sufficient and proper solution. It is not necessary or worthwhile to devote a lot of energy to such problems. If we do not mind them, these problems will go away.

At other times, we might have to avoid problems if we are not ready to face them, like a soldier who must temporarily retreat or rest before battle. If your problem is too strong, sharp, and fresh in your mind, you may not have the strength to face it or to apply any training directly to pacify it. Facing it too soon might inflame the pain and make the problem more difficult than it needs to be. In that case, the proper way to work with it at least for the time being, will be to avoid thinking about it. Later, when you have regained your composure and mental strength, you should try to resolve the problem or release it through meditation.

However, for those of us with minds that are strong and wild, it will be helpful not only to see our problems, but also to feel and experience the pain deeply. If we are the kind of person who feels that we are almost always right and other people are wrong, our pride can blind us to our problems. So, immediately facing pain, rather than avoiding it, can touch the core of your life, bring you back to your senses, and focus your attention in the right direction.

Sometimes avoidance is the best approach for the past hurts. Even if you have a residue of pain, the effect may be diminished if the negative experience is followed by a strong positive one. In that case, the problem may be somewhat neutralized. Then, instead of recreating the problem, it is probably best to just go on with the positive experience.

Getting Started

Over the centuries spirituality has developed a vast reservoir of knowledge about the mind. Especially, as we begin to learn meditation, all the suggestions and ideas may feel overwhelming. It is best to keep our practice simple. Set attainable goals and strive for them with positive energy. Do not worry about the difficulties, but instead feel glad about any benefits that come. Even negative experiences or so-called shortcomings can be a benefit if we view them positively.

When meditating we should relax and let go, rather than chasing our worries and desires. We usually sit down to meditate, but much of what we learn about meditation can be carried into all our daily activities. Words are necessary to describe how to meditate and how to bring the right attitude to our lives. However, the important thing is to practise and feel, without being overly concerned about concepts, categories or rules. Be patient and open, and work with what your own life brings to you.

Choosing a Place

The best place to practise spiritual training in healing is a peaceful, pleasant place where there are few distractions, where the mind can be calm and the body comfortable, and where we can feel alert, spacious and happy.

Sages of the past have praised a variety of places, depending on the character of the practitioner, the practice, and the season. Among the favoured solitary locations are those that have a clear, far-reaching view, like the lap of a prosperous field. Some practitioners have found solace in the forest, among the trees and wild animals and birds singing their ageless song of joy and playing free from fear. Others suggest training by the ocean with its dancing, ever-changing waves or a river with its mighty, natural flow. Still others have trained in the dry caves of empty valleys where there is an atmosphere of sublime peace.

If we do not live in such natural settings, we should find a pleasant place in our own home space, make the best of it, and rejoice.

Choose the quietest room or corner of a room of your home, during a time when there will be few disturbances from the telephone, children, roommates, spouse or friends. Then feel good: good about the place, the time, and the opportunity to have this place and time. Arouse joy at this chance to realize the spiritual meaning of your life.

Generally, it is better for beginners to practise alone, in a place that presents no obstructions. After gaining strength in the training, we can seek harder situations that require more tolerance and discipline — with obstacles such as disturbances from people or noise from traffic — to strengthen ourselves in using the hardships that come our way. Finally, when we are ready, we can practise dwelling in the worst situations, with all kinds of mental temptation and emotional turmoil. By practising diligently in this way, eventually we will be able to face and transform any situation into a source of strength without losing our peaceful mind. Wherever we live will then become a palace of enlightenment and purity. Every event will be a teaching. After that the place will not matter, the only need will be to choose a place where we can best serve others.

Choosing a Time

Although any time is fine for training, peace and calm are helpful for a beginner. Early morning is good, for then the day itself is fresh and the mind is clear. However, some might feel relaxed and ready to meditate in the evening. Choose a time, observe it regularly, and be happy with it. If you can, allow nothing to interfere with your regular practice.

Whatever meditation or healing exercise we do, we should give ourselves to it. We should not dream about the future or make plans in our heads. Do not run after the past or grasp at the present. All kinds of thoughts or mental experiences may arise during meditation, but instead of grasping at them, let them come and go. Meditate every day. Even if we meditate for a short time, the consistency will keep the contemplative experience alive and steady us on the path of healing.

How long should we meditate? Your mind is the healer, so the answer depends on your needs and abilities. You could meditate for a few minutes, for twenty minutes or for an hour. Do not be overly concerned with time, but rather consider what feels right.

It is especially good to practise when we are happy, healthy, and relatively free of problems. Then, when we face suffering which will certainly come, we will have the skillful means ready to apply. Unfortunately, it takes the experience of suffering for many of us to turn our minds towards spiritual solutions. When we are in the midst of pain and confusion, we may have less clarity, energy and opportunity for training.

Posture

The essential goal of any of the various postures for meditating is to relax the muscles and open the channels in the body so that energy and breath can flow naturally through them. Whatever posture makes our body straight and relaxed, but not stiff, will produce a natural flow of energy and allow the mind to be calm and flexible. The purpose of the physical postures is summarized in this popular Tibetan saying:

"If your body is straight, your channels will be straight.

If your channels are straight, your mind will be straight."

One of the most popular meditation positions is called the *lotus posture*, in which one sits cross-legged on the floor with the right foot on the left thigh and the left foot on the right thigh. Most westerners find the *half-lotus* easier, with one ankle resting on the fold of the opposite leg. If you sit on a small cushion, your torso will be raised up a bit in a way that you may find it open and relaxed. Your hands are placed on your lap, right hand over left with tips of thumbs touching, and palms up.

The elbows should be slightly away from the body, in a natural, wing-like position, instead of being cramped or pressed inward. The chin is lowered to allow the neck to bend slightly, so that it feels natural to focus the eyes a yard or two in front, at the level of the tip of the nose. The tip of the tongue gently touching the upper palate. The most important element of all is to keep the spine straight.

Some people may find the postures very difficult if they have back problems. You may want to sit on a chair to meditate, but make sure the chair allows you to keep your spine straight rather than slouching. Whatever posture you choose, remember that the purpose is not to be uncomfortable. The Buddha himself, after years of experimenting with ascetic practices, gave up mortification of the body. You should be comfortable enough so that your mind can relax and concentrate.

It is best to meditate in a sitting posture, but really our mind is capable of healing wherever we are and under any circumstance, as long as we are aware.

Relaxation

To release the struggles of our mind – the conceptual and emotional pressures that grip us, we should relax the tightness of our muscles when we meditate. If tension is gathered anywhere in your muscles, bring awareness to that area and release the tightness. Relaxation provides a calm atmosphere in which we can light the candle of healing energy. However, relaxation does not mean indulging in a lazy, careless, semiconscious, or sleepy state of mind. At times we may need to rest and be sleepy, but the most effective meditation is to be awake and alert. This is the way to touch our peaceful, joyous nature.

Allow yourself to stay relaxed in the transition from meditation back to your daily routine. Get up slowly and ease your mind into your activities. This way, you bring a spacious mind into your life.

Creating Mental Space

Few of us give ourselves completely to what we are doing. We bring our job problems home and so have no chance to enjoy our home life. Then we take our home problems to work and cannot devote ourselves to our job. While trying to meditate, we fondle our mental images and feelings, which gives us no real chance to concentrate. We end up having no life to live, as we are always dwelling in the past or future.

If we cluttered up our homes with too much furniture, we would have no place to live. If our minds are cluttered with plans, concerns, thoughts and emotional patterns, we have no space for our true selves.

Many people feel their lives are too crowded to meditate. Even when they have time at home to meditate, they feel too distracted. To bring our full attention and energy to our home lives, and to meditation, we need mental space.

We can consciously create space for ourselves. We can decide to leave our worries about work behind us. If it is helpful we could visualize these worries in the form of papers and computers that are safely back in the office. We could even imagine borderlines separating our work lives from home. Or we could create a protective tent of energy or light in our minds, enclosing us in our home and granting complete privacy for what we are doing now.

Meditation can be a haven of warmth and space, but we may feel resistance to meditating or think of it as a chore. One way to create an open and relaxed feeling is to go back to the atmosphere of childhood.

Touching childhood memories can help us open up. As a meditation, go back to a positive memory from when you were young and had few worries, passions or pressures. The exact memory is not as important as the feeling of space and freedom. Rather than standing outside the memory and thinking about it, allow the feeling to expand and go within it. Experience the feeling and remain in it, without other thoughts. Let yourself feel and be one with yourself as a child. The past and present, the child and "me," all are one in spacious union. Contemplate and rest within this open feeling again and again. Finally, bring that feeling to the present moment of your life.

If bad experiences in your childhood come up instead of peaceful and spacious feelings, then you can use the approach outlined later in the visualisation exercises to purify, nourish, and heal the injured image, and visualize that your inner child has become happy, healthy and cheerful.

Since childhood, we have learned and experienced a lot of wonderful things in this generous world. However, it is easy to be caught up in today's frantic lifestyle. We can become like silkworms trapped by their own silk. We reach a stage where we suffocate ourselves with our own views, feelings, habits and reactions.

Thinking back, we remember that as children, a day seemed to last for a long time, more like the way we experience a month now. A year was so long there was no end to it. Gradually our perceptions changed.

Our preoccupations, concepts and attachments grew day by day. Now the open space is no longer there in our minds. As we grew, we felt time become shorter and shorter, and now a year passes in the blink of an eye. It is not because time actually became shorter, but because we do not have the mental space to feel open and free. We run around at full speed, and crowd our minds with a houseful of thoughts, concepts and emotions. When our minds are calm, we feel every minute of time, but if our minds chase after everything going on around us, we feel that the day has ended before it has even begun.

We can contact this spacious feeling anytime, for example, if we are having difficulty sitting down to meditate, or whenever we want to bring a sense of freedom and enjoyment to our lives. To reach the child within us, we can also enjoy childhood activities — games like juggling, and jump rope — or appreciate trees, flowers, water and the beauty of nature. We can look at the night sky and stars through the eyes of wonder that we had as a child, and enjoy being out in the night air as we did then. These feelings will help us to enlarge our perception of time and enable our mental space to be open and free like the carefree days of childhood.

Spending time in solitude with nature, especially watching the infinite space of the sky from a mountaintop, will also help us make our minds spacious. But the most effective way to open up a peaceful space in our minds is meditation. Instead of crowding our minds with negative views and feelings, if we can get back to the skylike nature of the mind, a dawn of peace and wisdom can then arise.

Breathing

In any kind of meditation, it is important to breathe naturally and calmly. Contemplation of our breathing, the mind's awareness of the breath, in and out, is in itself a foundation for realizing our true nature.

Highly experienced meditators use this approach as a means to realize selflessness. Although in our healing exercises we will not be concerned with going beyond concepts of self, awareness of breathing can be very useful for other purposes. For example, it is a good way to calm ourselves, focus our minds, and establish a flow of energy that enables healing to progress.

At the beginning, you may feel it is impossible to concentrate fully on the simple act of breathing in and out. It can be shocking to see how fast the mind moves. Do not worry about this. Gently bring your consciousness back to your breathing and give your complete awareness to this. By just allowing our minds to touch and unite with the natural process of breathing, we can release stress and feel more relaxed.

The contemplation of breathing is important in the higher practice of meditation. But for now, consider using the contemplation of breathing as preliminary to any healing exercise. Awareness of breathing is also a very powerful method to release any difficult emotion that has us in a vice-like grip.

A particularly helpful technique is to concentrate on your relaxed exhalation. In this way, grasping is relaxed.

Visualization

One of the best tools in healing is visualization, which can transform our mental patterns from negative to positive. Some beginners at meditation regard visualization as a difficult or unusual mental activity. Actually, it is quite natural, for we think in images all the time. When we think of our friends or family, or imagine ourselves at a lovely beach or mountain lake, we see these images in our minds quite vividly. In meditation we visualize for a particular purpose, but the mental process is the same. With practice, we can get better at it.

For instance, some professional athletes visualize to improve their performance and realize their full potential.

Positive images inspire all sorts of people in all kinds of activities. The most important point in visualizing is to call up the positive image with warmth and whole-heartedness. Give your full attention to the mental objects, become totally absorbed in it. Allow the mind and the object to become one. If we see the image in our minds half-heartedly or in a distracted way, our concentration is limited. Then it is as if we were staring blankly at an object just with our eyes, instead of with our whole being.

For beginners, especially, the key is to feel the presence of what you are imagining. Your visualization does not need to be elaborate or detailed;

for it is the clarity and stability of your mental images that matters.

Concentration

For any spiritual training or mental activity, we need concentration. Learning how to concentrate makes our minds strong, clear and calm. Concentration protects our inner wisdom, like a candle flame sheltered from the wind.

For spiritualists concentration on an object with spiritual significance will generate positive energy, blessings, and virtuous *karma*. However, we can train our minds to concentrate by practising on virtually anything, whether it is a physical object or a mental image, regardless of whether it is spiritually meaningful.

If we are unable to concentrate our minds, even years of practice will yield little insight, despite the merits of the effort.

The first step in developing concentration is to bring our restless mind down to earth.

Once we feel grounded mentally, we can deepen our ability to concentrate. Experienced meditators sometimes practice visualizing a long, narrow pipe and using their imagination to look through it.

Another mental exercise involves concentrating on a single tiny spot instead of a larger image.

If we need to work on concentration, awaken our minds, or sharpen our senses, we should focus for a while on developing mental discipline. However, often our minds are too discriminative and sensitive. If your mind feels trapped or suppressed, it is best not to force it rigidly into concentration. Those who feel burdened by mental stress and worries can find it very soothing to open up their awareness instead of focusing in a concentrated manner.

Opening

One way to break through the feeling of emotional suffocation is to find a place high where you can have a far-reaching view, such as the top of a mountain or a building. If the sky is very clear, sit with your back to the sun. Concentrate on the depth of the open sky without moving your eyes. Slowly exhale and experience the openness, vastness, and voidness.

Feel that the whole universe has become one in the vast openness. Think that all phenomena — trees, mountains and rivers have dissolved spontaneously into the open sky. Your mind and body has dissolved there too. All have vanished like clouds disappearing from the sky. Relax in the feeling of openness, free from boundaries and limitations. This exercise is not only effective for calming the mind but can also generate higher realization.

If you cannot go to such a place, choose any spot from which you have a good view of the sky or from which you can at least visualize the open sky.

Merging in Oneness

Merging in oneness means being one with whatever we are experiencing. It sometimes helps in the beginning to describe oneness in words: for example, that it is like being a swimmer at one with the vast ocean. But actually words are not necessary for the experience of oneness and openness. We simply let go of our struggles and relax the need to put labels such as "good" or "bad" on experiences. We drop expectations about how we should feel or want to feel, and instead allow ourselves to be with the feeling or to go within it. By merging with experiences or feelings, the character of experience can change. By allowing ourselves to be just as we are in the present moment, the walls of our discriminations and sensitivities will soften, or fall away altogether. Our minds and hearts open, and our energy flows. This is a powerful healing.

Mindfulness

Learning to live in the moment is a great and powerful skill that will help us in everything we do. To "be here now," relaxed and engaged in whatever we are doing, is to be alive and healthy. In Buddhism, the awareness of what is happening right now is called mindfulness.

In everyday life, mindfulness is an alert mind that is aware of every aspect that is going on, and what to do, without being scattered. In meditation, mindfulness is giving ourselves completely to our breathing, or whatever the exercise is.

Mindfulness is giving full attention to the present, without worries about the past or the future. So often, we borrow trouble from the future by constantly thinking about what might befall us tomorrow, instead of dealing with one day at a time.

In spirituality the emphasis is on this very moment. We can guide our minds to live in the present. To do this, we need to firmly establish a habit of total attention to what we are doing now. For every undertaking, we should consciously decide to keep other ideas, feelings and activities out and give ourselves to what we are doing.

To be mindful does not mean to become emotionally intense or to stir up hosts of concepts in order to watch what we are thinking or doing. On the contrary, the mind is relaxed and calm, and therefore sharply aware of every event as it is, without conceptual and emotional struggle. However, when we notice that our mind is wandering, we should gently but firmly bring ourselves back to the present and to what we are doing. For most of us, especially in the beginning, we may need to do this again and again.

Even if we are instructed in meditation or spiritual training, we need mindfulness and awareness, otherwise the mind will run about like a wild beast, unable to remain focused or at rest even for a few moments. Then what will we gain from our mere physical participation in meditation?

The fruit of mindfulness is the protection it provides in all kinds of turmoil and difficulty.

With mindfulness and awareness, we learn to be patient or to act, as the occasion calls for. Patience then becomes a transforming energy.

The practice of mindfulness should not result in stress. If it does, it may be a sign that we are trying too hard — that we are grasping at "mindfulness" itself, that we need to relax a little and be less self-conscious.

By remaining in a relaxed and spacious mood, we can live in a spontaneous stream of mindfulness and awareness. Our minds will become steadier, instead of constantly fragmenting into scattered thoughts and wildly chasing the past or future. After a while, our concentration will improve and we will find it easier to meditate. Learning how to enjoy and be in the present moment leads to openness and timeless time. By being mindful, we find the peace within ourselves.

TITLES IN THE SERIES

All You Wanted to Know About

Happiness

Relaxation

Spirituality

Self-Motivation

Spiritual Healing

Love & Relationships